—— joy redefined ——

LOVING OTHERS

Printed in the United States of America.

First Printing, 2018

ISBN 978-1-942854-61-6

Joyce Meyer Ministries
P.O. Box 655
Fenton, Missouri 63026
joycemeyer.org

LOVING OTHERS

Throughout history there has been a tendency to make Christianity all about a system of beliefs and religious practices. But real Christianity is about relationship, not religion. And it can be summed up in two commands: Love God and love people.

Luke 10:27 says, **"...You shall love the Lord your God with all your heart, and with all your soul, and with all your strength, and with all your mind; and your neighbor as yourself."**

All throughout the Bible, believers are encouraged to abound in love and increase in love. And love is one of my favorite subjects to teach on! Learning the importance of walking in love changed my life because it finally got my mind off of me and onto what I can do for others.

The truth is, the way we treat others is the truest test of what we really believe.

In this book, I want to encourage you to live your life the way Jesus did, loving others. As you take this journey, you'll find you are happier than you've ever been when you're focused on helping people.

So if you're wondering how to be happy, don't look in the mirror. Just look around you.

GOD WANTS US TO KNOW EXACTLY WHAT TO DO TO PLEASE HIM . . .

AND HOW
TO HAVE A
WONDERFUL LIFE.

CHAPTER ONE

God's Passion

God is love—it's who He is and what He does —and His passion is helping hurting people. As believers in Christ, our purpose in life is to walk in love and follow the example of Christ. Helping others, being a blessing and adding value to other people's lives is what it means to walk in love.

Ephesians 5:1-2 says, **Therefore become imitators of God [copy Him and follow His example], as well-beloved children [imitate their father]; and walk continually in love [that is, value one another—practice empathy and compassion, unselfishly** *seeking the best for others], just as Christ also loved you and gave Himself up for us, an offering and sacrifice to God [slain for you, so that it became] a sweet fragrance.*

How do we imitate God? We walk in love. And that's what I want to help you learn to do. I want to show you how to really live as a Christian, so that others will follow your example. In the process, you'll experience the joy of living like Christ.

Isaiah 1:16-17 (NKJV) gives us a picture of what a Christian lifestyle looks like:

> *"Wash yourselves,*
> *make yourselves clean;*
> *Put away the evil of your*
> *doings from before My eyes.*
> *Cease to do evil,*

Learn to do good;
Seek justice,
Rebuke the oppressor;
Defend the fatherless,
Plead for the widow."

This isn't Isaiah's advice—this is *the word of the Lord.* I'm not mentioning this so you will respond out of fear; knowing these instructions are from God should be a comfort. God wants us to know exactly what to do to please Him and how to have a wonderful life. He's very clear about what He wants to see in our lives.

———————————

WHAT IS REAL LOVE?

Jesus gave us the greatest example of how to walk in love. He is our perfect and holy Savior…and He willingly gave His life for us, took all of our sin upon Himself, and shed His blood so we could have a personal relationship with God. Through Christ, we become the righteousness of God! (See 2 Corinthians 5:21.)

Salvation is God's gift to us.
Choosing to live a lifestyle of
walking in love is our gift to Him.

I believe we live in a love-starved society. Everywhere you go, there are probably people who haven't had the right kind of love in their lives, making them insecure and fearful. Many addictions happen as a result of this lack of love—people feel empty, they have emotional pain, they think they are worthless, and they are desperate for relief.

It's very painful to feel you are worthless and have no purpose in life. And God wants to put us—His children—into the lives of those who are hurting so He can love them into wholeness through us.

Love is not just a feeling, a theory or a nice word. It's action—it's the way you treat others, what you do for others. Love will always cost you something: time, energy, money, giving up your pride, doing what's right when you don't feel like it, keeping a good attitude when you don't get your way.

Loving the way God loves means you love when there's nothing in it for you; it's all about giving out and not expecting anything in return. We're called to *outreach*, not in-reach.

> *Real love is about dying to self*
> *and living to love others.*

The Bible describes love in 1 Corinthians 13:4-8. It says love…

- **Endures with patience and serenity**

- Is kind and thoughtful

- **Is not jealous or envious**

- Does not brag and is not proud or arrogant

- **Is not rude**

- Is not self-seeking, overly sensitive or easily angered

- **Does not take into account a wrong endured—it doesn't keep score**

- Does not rejoice at injustice, but rejoices when right and truth prevail

- **Bears all things, regardless of what comes**

- Believes all things, looking for the best in each one

- **Hopes all things, remaining steadfast during difficult times**

- Endures all things without weakening

- **Never fails, fades or ends!**

This passage of Scripture gives us a clear picture of what love looks like. And we were created by God to be loved by Him and to love others.

THE CYCLE OF LOVE

There's a cycle to love. We need to understand it so we can really love others the way God loves us. It's so amazing that God willingly loves us with an unconditional love. And He loved us before we ever loved Him.

Colossians 2:13 says, ***When you were dead in your sins and in the uncircumcision of your flesh (worldliness, manner of life), God made you alive together with Christ, having [freely] forgiven us all our sins.***

So the first step is recognizing that God loves you, accepting His love by faith. Then you begin to love Him back. And then you can let His love flow through you to others.

We have to go through these steps because we can't give love away if we don't have it. I remember when I struggled to believe God really loved me because of the guilt and shame I carried from the past abuse I'd experienced. I would say out loud several times a day, "God loves me!" This was my declaration of faith about God's love for me, and as I did it day after day, eventually it became real to me and I received His love.

Once I reached this point in my relationship with God, it was easier to love others and stop thinking so much about myself.

The bottom line here is, the only way you can have a happy, powerful life is to be like Jesus—to get your mind off yourself and do something for someone else. Helping people . . . being a blessing and adding value to other people's lives is what it means to walk in love and follow the example of Jesus.

IF WE'RE IN A HURRY ALL THE TIME, WE CAN'T BE SENSITIVE TO THE HOLY SPIRIT.

WE'VE GOT TO
SLOW DOWN
ENOUGH TO BE
ABLE TO HEAR
WHAT GOD IS
SAYING TO US.

CHAPTER TWO

The True Source of Happiness

No one sets out to live a miserable life, yet it seems so many end up feeling that way. Oftentimes, when we try to figure out what is making us unhappy, our thoughts center on someone or something else. Other people—our spouse, our bossy neighbor, our wayward child—they are the problem. Or we think if we just had a different job, a bigger house, more money, or some other circumstance, *then* we could be happy.

But the real problem isn't someone or something else. The root of the problem is the attitude of our heart and our perspective

—a selfish, self-centered, "What about me?!" mindset.

THE ROOT OF OUR PROBLEM

Most of us have all heard about Sodom and Gomorrah and the sin of the people within those cities. Both cities were destroyed by God because the people were so wicked. And if you ask people what their sin was, most people will say sexual perversion. That was certainly one of the ways they sinned, but that was not the real *root* of their problem—rather it was the *fruit* of their problem.

Many people have bad fruit in their lives that comes from the root of selfishness. For example, there are people who have the fruit of broken or dysfunctional relationships, but the root of their problem is selfishness. There are people who have a fruit of loneliness, yet they struggle to have healthy relationships, and the root of their problem is selfishness.

You can't have good relationships if you're selfish because nobody wants to be in a relationship where everything is one-sided. We must understand that it's not all about us. If you're a parent, you may have told your children, "The world doesn't revolve around you." If we're honest, we would all say we need this reminder often.

In Ezekiel 16:49, the prophet says, ***Look, this was the iniquity of your sister Sodom: She and her daughter had pride, fullness of food, and abundance of idleness; neither***

***did she strengthen the hand of the poor
and needy*** (NKJV).

Pride, overabundance of food, prosperous
ease, and idleness were the lifestyle of
Sodom . . . ***neither did she strengthen
the hand of the poor and the needy.*** So
what was Sodom's real sin? It was idolatry,
indifference to the poor, having too much
and not sharing it with anybody—a selfish,
self-centered lifestyle.

THE FUEL THAT DRIVES OUR MISERY

We live in a society that drives us to selfishness. It seems almost everywhere we look, there's a message of some kind telling us we need *more* to be satisfied ... more stuff or more things to make us more like the images we see on TV and in magazines. It's amazing what we think we need to have to be truly satisfied.

This is such a miserable way to live because it keeps the focus on "me." And putting yourself <u>above</u> others is at the heart of nearly everyone's misery. The pull of selfishness is very strong, and I've learned that if we're going to counteract it, we must have an aggressive, on-purpose love walk.

I stress "on purpose" because being self-centered is a natural mindset unless we consciously choose to think about others and then do something to help them or simply make their day better. You can't wait for a feeling to motivate you.

I like to say that love is
"a set of behaviors
you choose to operate in."
Love is a choice!

So, if you're going to walk in love, then you're going to have to make lots of decisions every day, all day long, to think of others—before yourself—and treat them well.

———————————————

SLOW DOWN AND
CHOOSE TO LOVE

The pace of life today is often fast and hectic with many things happening at once. Instead of rushing through the day, trying to do three things at once, we need to slow down and live in the moment. Because if we're in a hurry all the time, we can't be sensitive to the Holy Spirit. We've got to slow down enough to be able to hear what God is saying to us.

When I think about how Jesus walked through His daily life on Earth, I'm sure He didn't get stressed-out and rush around in an anxious state of mind. He was always at peace in His soul, and He always did what He was led to do by the Holy Spirit.

John 5:19 (NIV) says, *" . . . The Son can do nothing by himself; he can only do what he sees his Father doing, because whatever the Father does the Son also does."*

Many times when He was walking from one place to the next, He would stop and help others along the way. He wasn't so focused on getting somewhere that He missed opportunities to meet needs in the process of taking His journey.

In Matthew 20:32, Jesus had an encounter with two blind men. When they called to Him for mercy, the New International Version says, *Jesus stopped and called them . . .* There's an important message here: STOP!

If you don't remember anything else you've read so far, I want you to remember to

BEING SELFLESS

IS THE KEY TO

LIVING WITH . . .

REAL JOY,
FULFILLMENT
AND PURPOSE.

STOP! Do you believe that there could be needs all around us, but we're oblivious to them because we're in such a hurry doing *our* thing and going where *we* want to go? The Bible says we're to watch and pray, and I really think that we need to pay more attention to that particular direction from Scripture. We need to pay attention...to watch for needs and be aware of what people are going through.

Here's another example we can learn from. Mark 10:46-49 (NIV) says, **Then they came to Jericho. As Jesus and his disciples, together with a large crowd, were leaving the city, a blind man, Bartimaeus (which means "son of Timaeus"), was sitting by the roadside begging. When he heard that it was Jesus of Nazareth, he began to shout, "Jesus, Son of David, have mercy on me!"**

Many rebuked him and told him to be quiet, but he shouted all the more, "Son of David, have mercy on me!" Jesus stopped and said, "Call him. . . ."

Just as Jesus was never too busy to slow down and help people in need, we need to do the same.

———————————————————

THE REWARD OF A SELFLESS LIFESTYLE

Being selfless is the key to living with real joy, fulfillment and purpose. This is a life-changing revelation I've received as I've studied the Word of God; it's literally transformed me from being selfish, miserable and brokenhearted to having real peace, healing and happiness.

The process of changing from selfish and self-centered to focusing on others wasn't easy; in fact, it was painful at times. But the benefits of walking in love are *much greater* than the misery of just living for myself.

Now I continually work at walking in love because I would still have a tendency to be selfish if I didn't fight it every day of my life.

When the Bible encourages us to fight the good fight of faith (see 1 Timothy 6:12), one of the things it's talking about is fighting our own selfish, self-centered nature.

In John 13:34, Jesus says, ***"I am giving you a new commandment, that you love one another. Just as I have loved you, so you too are to love one another."*** How did Jesus love us? He willingly gave Himself up for us when He gave His life on the cross. That was a totally unselfish act of unconditional love!

———————————————————

MAKING A DIFFERENCE, ONE GOOD CHOICE AT A TIME

Psalm 89:14 says, ***Righteousness and justice are the foundation of Your throne; lovingkindness and truth go before You.***

This is a powerful scripture! God's throne is upheld through righteousness and justice. He is righteous and just—that's His character; it makes Him who He is. As His children, we will live in His righteousness and justice. We'll be living examples of how to live the way Jesus did.

As I said before, I used to be very unhappy. I was hard to get along with, manipulative, controlling…and I wasted day after day full of self-pity. This attitude and selfish mindset caused me to make bad choices for many years.

Galatians 6:7 says, *... **Whatever a man sows,
this and this only is what he will reap.*** In
other words, our actions have consequences,
and they are based on the type of "seed"
we sow, or decisions we make day in and day
out.

When I faced the truth about myself—why
I was so unhappy—I cried for several days.
But it was good for me to finally realize the
truth because it was the beginning of my
turnaround. The truth of God's Word set
me free!

Things didn't change overnight; I had to learn
to take responsibility for my choices and
start making right decisions, one day at a
time. Over time, I sowed a lot of good seeds,
and it eventually got me to the place where
I have a more positive attitude and live with

God's peace in my soul.

I want to encourage you with this: No matter how many bad seeds you've sown, if you will start sowing good seeds, good will always overcome evil! (See Romans 12:21.) The key is making a determined decision that with God's help, you're going to do what's right and keep it up. And loving others is always a right choice!

THE MORE YOU
TRUST GOD TO
MEET YOUR NEEDS,
THE MORE YOU'LL
BE FREE TO
HELP OTHERS . . .

AND THE HAPPIER

YOU'LL BE.

CHAPTER THREE

The Simple Solution

The world is full of lonely, hurting people who are hungry for the love of God and the hope that is only found in Jesus. I want to encourage you to get rid of a "What about me?" mindset and instead pray, "God, show me someone who needs a blessing. Show me someone who needs a blessing. Show me someone I can help."

We all have room to grow in our relationship with God, and learning how to reach out to others is a big part of that process. Selfishness and always trying to meet your own needs puts you in a position of weakness. But the more you trust God to meet your needs, the more you'll be free to help others . . . and the happier you'll be.

Imagine how different the world would be if everyone would just do one nice thing to help someone else every day. It can be so simple to put a smile on someone's face. Give a compliment, give something away, take the time to listen, open a door for someone, let someone go before you in line at the store . . . the list could go on and on.

Make it your business to regularly reach out to people around you, encouraging them and meeting their needs as you are able to do it. Be determined each day to do at least one thing for someone else that makes their life better.

Trust me: You'll discover that serving God

by loving others is the most wonderful,
exciting thing you can do!

———————————————

GIVE YOUR "LITTLE" TO GOD

Some people don't do anything because they don't think they can really make a difference. But that's a lie from the enemy! When we look for people with needs, the Holy Spirit will lead us to bless people—in both little things and big things. Many times the little things make a bigger difference than we think they will.

Jesus' life is considered remarkable not just for walking on water or raising the dead, but also because of the little things He did for others ... the kind of things that many times in our own daily life we might consider to be insignificant. Yet, Jesus did them as an example for us.

For instance, on the night of His betrayal,

after the Passover Feast, Jesus poured a basin of water, wrapped a towel around His waist, and began to wash His disciples' feet (see John 13). This was so remarkable because in those days, the servants who washed people's feet were likely considered the lowliest servants in the household. Yet, there was Jesus, the Savior of the world, washing His disciples' feet!

His message to them was to love one another by being a servant.

———————————————

BE A LIFETIME
LEARNER OF LOVE

When it comes to growing spiritually and becoming more like Jesus, we need to be lifetime learners. Because throughout our lives, there will always be more we can learn about walking in love and doing what's right in God's eyes.

Isaiah 1:17 (NIV) says, **Learn to do right; seek justice. Defend the oppressed. Take up the cause of the fatherless; plead the case of the widow.**

This scripture tells us to *seek justice.* The word *seek* means "to crave, pursue and go after *with all your might.*" It's a very strong word in the Bible. *Seeking justice* is not just talking about justice for you; it's talking about justice for the oppressed. In other words, when you see people who are not being treated right, you *seek* and find a way to help them and to make things right in their lives.

———————————————

YOU CAN MAKE WRONG THINGS RIGHT

Every time we see something wrong, our first response should be to pray about it, and our second response should be to ask, "What can I do about this?" God did not create us for inactivity and passivity. He created us to be zealous, enthusiastic and passionate. He gave us gifts and talents for His glory . . . to help other people.

God calls us to relieve the oppressed and correct the oppressor, to defend the fatherless, and plead for the widow. And as we are obedient to God, we will show others how to seek God's justice.

Hebrews 11:6 teaches us that ***without faith it is impossible to [walk with God and]***

please Him, for whoever comes [near] to God must [necessarily] believe that God exists and that He rewards those who [earnestly and diligently] seek Him. And Isaiah 1:19 (NIV) says God's promise to us is this: ***If you are willing and obedient, you will eat the good things of the land.***

Being a Christian really is simple because it's a lifestyle…it's living according to what God's Word teaches us is true and right. It's about actively pursuing a personal relationship with God and then reaching out to others to show His love to them. I like to say it's "doing life with God" because you consider God's ways in everything you do. You get involved with people as He shows you how to walk in love.

BLESSED TO BE A BLESSING

Abraham is a great example of one who was blessed by God, and therefore, he was a blessing to others. Genesis 12:2 says, ***And I will make you a great nation, and I will bless you [abundantly], and make your name great (exalted, distinguished); and you shall be a blessing [a source of great good to others].***

God told Abraham, "I will bless you and I will make you *a blessing [a source of great good to others.* He wants to do the same for us. I pray for God to show me how to help someone every day. I want to be a blessing everywhere I go!

When the love of God is in our hearts, it compels us to do what's right. And the more

IF WE SEE OUR
BLESSINGS AS
OPPORTUNITIES TO
HELP OTHERS, OUR
FOCUS REMAINS ON
GOD'S HEART . . .

HIS DESIRE TO
HELP OTHERS . . .
AND WE EXPERIENCE
THE JOY OF BEING
A BLESSING.

we fall in love with Jesus, the more we're going to do what He wants us to do, whether it's comfortable or convenient or not. The less we will think, *What about me?,* the more we will walk in love toward others.

When we have an abundance of things, it's easy to become selfish and self-centered, always thinking about what we want, how we feel, and what we think. But if we see our blessings as opportunities to help others, our focus remains on God's heart...His desire to help others...and we experience the joy of being a blessing. God wants to bless us *so we can be a blessing.*

––––––––––––––––––––

GENEROSITY: THE PREREQUISITE FOR A HAPPY LIFE

Giving to the poor, feeding the hungry, and helping to meet a simple physical need are things many of us can easily do. To us it's a little thing to give a donation to a good cause, whether the amount is large or small, but it means a whole lot to the person who gets relief from the aid that money helped to provide.

Sometimes we can meet a need by giving things we have, like clothing, furniture, or an appliance. We can also bless others by giving our time to just listen to them. There are many lonely people around us who would be so happy if someone would spend a few hours with them. Maybe you can serve someone by cleaning their house, babysitting for free, or running an errand for them. And an encouraging word or compliment is something we can all give. It's amazing how powerful a few words can be!

There are many ways to help others. We just need to be willing to give what we have as the Holy Spirit puts the prompting in our heart to do it.

The more we understand God's love for us and receive His love, the more we will be moved with compassion for others. Matthew 9:36 (NKJV) says that when Jesus saw the multitudes, ***He was moved with compassion for them, because they were weary and scattered, like sheep having no shepherd.***

God is passionate about helping the

oppressed and needy, and we should be the same way. In John 15:12, Jesus says, ***"This is My commandment, that you love and unselfishly seek the best for one another, just as I have loved you."*** God is calling us to walk in love. And one of the best things I can teach you is to find somebody who is hurting and try to make a difference in their life.

THROUGH OUR
RELATIONSHIP
WITH CHRIST, WE
FIND THE STRENGTH
AND ABILITY TO
LOVE OTHERS . . .

EVEN WHEN IT
SEEMS TO COST
MORE THAN WE
THINK WE CAN GIVE.

CHAPTER FOUR

A Lifestyle of Loving Others

As Christians, we're destined to be molded into the image of Jesus (see Romans 8:29). He is the greatest example of what it means to love others and live an unselfish life.

In Mark 8:34, Jesus says, *. . . **"If anyone wishes to follow Me [as My disciple], he must deny himself [set aside selfish interests], and take up his cross [expressing a willingness to endure whatever may come] and follow Me [believing in Me, conforming to My example in living and, if need be, suffering or perhaps dying because of faith in Me]."***

This verse makes it clear that we're supposed to put other people first, and that God expects us to treat everyone well. When we do, we glorify Him, like Jesus did when He gave His life for us!

Acts 10:38 says that ***God anointed Jesus of Nazareth with the Holy Spirit and with great power; and He went around doing good and healing all who were oppressed by the devil, because God was with Him.*** Jesus got up every day, He spent time with God, and He basically walked around the countryside meeting needs. It was so simple, yet He led the most influential life in the history of mankind.

IT'S WORTH THE COST!

As I said in the previous chapter, loving others is not always easy because it costs us something—time, money, energy—and sometimes it's inconvenient. But through our relationship with Christ, we find the strength and ability to love others, even when it seems to cost more than we think we can give.

I remember when God spoke to my heart that Dave and I should take care of my parents in their old age. This meant we would move them to the city where we live, buy a home for them and provide the care they needed. This was so hard for me because my father had abused me throughout my childhood, and my mother had abandoned me by not doing anything to stop it. But God gave me the grace to do it, and one of the results was that my father accepted Christ as his Savior before he died. This is one of the greatest victories I've ever had!

God is faithful to give us His love, grace and wisdom to reach out and be a blessing as His Spirit leads us to do so. And when we do, we end up receiving more joy and peace in the process!

It's important to be led by the Holy Spirit and use wisdom so you can be healthy emotionally, mentally and physically while you're helping others. The key to maintaining this balance is keeping your relationship with God your number one priority and doing what He puts in your heart to do.

YOUR MOTIVES MATTER

God wants us to do good deeds and help others, but He wants us to do it with a pure heart. The truth is, our motives for doing what we do matter more to Him than what we do.

In 1 Samuel 16, when the prophet was searching for the man God would anoint to be the next king of Israel, verse 7 says: *"...The Lord does not look at the things people look at. People look at the outward appearance, but the Lord looks at the heart"* (NIV). And 1 Corinthians 13 says we can give all we possess to the poor and suffer hardship for others, but if we don't have love, it is meaningless to God.

In Isaiah 58, God told His people that their

fasting was not producing any good fruit because their motives were wrong and they had wicked hearts. Verse 4 says, ***"The facts are that you fast only for strife and brawling and to strike with the fist of wickedness. You do not fast as you do today to make your voice heard on high."***

If we have a selfish mindset, our attitude about giving to others will be, *Well, I'll do something for you, but what are you going to do for me?* Or, *I do this for you, and I do that for you, and you don't do anything for me!* Even though we don't say it, if we think it, then we'll start having bad attitudes toward others.

Instead, God wants us to serve one another out of a pure heart, compelled by His love and a sincere desire to give. We should give to others as if we're doing it for God. Then we'll put our expectations in God and our attitude will be, *I'm expecting YOU to meet my needs, God.* That's when we can give to others unselfishly, with pure motives.

There's no better way to live because *God has unlimited ways to bless you and meet your needs.* But when you look to people to meet your needs, you're limiting Him in your life. Honestly, it's insulting to God when we go to people to get what only He can give us.

TRUSTING GOD POSITIONS US TO DO GOOD

Psalm 37:3 says, **Trust [rely on and have confidence] in the Lord and do good; dwell in the land and feed [securely] on His faithfulness.**

This verse tells us two things we must do at all times: trust God and do good. We can choose to trust God. The truth is, God is the only One we can completely trust to take care of us and do what's best for us at all times, in every situation.

In John 15:5, Jesus tells us, **"I am the vine; you are the branches. If you remain in me and I in you, you will bear much fruit; apart from me you can do nothing"** (NIV). The key to fulfilling the plan and purpose God has for

GOD WILL NEVER

TELL US TO DO

SOMETHING

WITHOUT . . .

GIVING US THE
ABILITY TO DO IT.

our lives is abiding in Christ. As we do, He will surely meet every need we have.

So don't make plans and pray for God to bless them, or make them work. Pray first and ask God to guide you in the plans you make. This is so important because God will always give us the ability to do what He tells us to do.

In Christ, you're able to meet other people's needs and put your trust in God to meet your needs. He will work through people as He chooses, and they may not be the ones you would expect to help you. In the same way, He may lead you to help someone you wouldn't normally think about helping.

Remember that God is perfect, and He is always right! He's smarter than we are, and the best thing we can do is humble ourselves before Him and get His direction for the way we live in every situation. When we do this, things always work out better than they would have if we just did them our way.

––––––––––––––––––––––––––––––––––––––

YOU CAN DO IT!

Go back to the description of love in 1 Corinthians 13 that's listed in chapter 1. If you're thinking, *There's no way I can live up to this list!* I want to tell you, "Yes, you can!" You can love others with the love of God because as a born-again Christian, you have everything you need to be like Jesus. God will never tell us to do something without giving us the ability to do it. We have to remember that we will be able to walk in love as we abide in Him (see John 15:5).

I realize it's not always easy to resist the temptation to be selfish, but 1 John 4:4 says that the Spirit of God in us is greater than our enemy. So, in Christ, you have the power you need to walk by faith and live a life of love.

Before I get into the ways you can practically love others, I want to say that it's important to understand that God is not expecting you to be perfect in your love walk or to do it in your own strength. He knows you can't do it without His help. He wants you to seek Him through prayer and studying His Word, and to lean on Him for the grace to do what He's asking you to do each day.

God IS love, so you can rest in the truth that He is patient with you, He's always with you, He believes in you, and He will not give up on you!

Let's consider three passages about doing good on purpose. Hebrews 13:16 (AMPC) encourages us, ***Do not forget or neglect to do kindness and good, to be generous and distribute and contribute to the needy [of*** *the church as embodiment and proof of fellowship], for such sacrifices are pleasing to God.* I like the fact Paul went to the church and said, "Now don't forget to do this." In other words, they knew to do it, but he reminded them to take action now and do it. Following his example, I'm saying to you today, "Don't forget to meet needs. I don't care if you have to write yourself notes. Don't forget to meet needs."

Start each day with a prayer, thanking God for another opportunity to live for Him and honor Him by loving the people you encounter as you go about your day. Then keep your eyes open for opportunities to meet needs and make someone else's life better. I promise you'll discover ways to be a blessing that will not only help others, but will also make you happier than you've ever been.

PRACTICAL WAYS
TO LOVE OTHERS

- Help a single mom who is overwhelmed with the daily responsibilities of parenting and needs a break by watching her children for a few hours.

- Become a foster parent or adopt a child.

- Adopt a widow or a widower who is lonely or needs help around the house. Offer companionship and practical help with daily needs, such as running errands or cleaning.

- Visit a nursing home.

- **Tutor children who need extra support with school work.**

- Donate your unused items to an organization that helps the needy in your area.

- **Instead of trading your old car in for a new one, prayerfully consider giving it to someone who needs a car but can't afford one.**

- Secretly pay someone's bill in a restaurant.

- **Carry gift certificates with you so you can bless people.**

- Offer transportation to somebody without a car or to someone who's having car trouble. Offer to go out of your way to pick them up.

- **Pay a month's rent or a utility bill for a single mom, a needy widow or for a family you know who's struggling financially.**

- Buy one month's groceries for an individual or family in need.

This list may give you ideas you can use, or it may inspire you to create your own list. Pray for God to open your eyes to ways you can help the people around you.